Poems For My Love

TIFFANY OSTENSON

authorHOUSE®

AuthorHouse™
1663 Liberty Drive
Bloomington, IN 47403
www.authorhouse.com
Phone: 1-800-839-8640

Published by AuthorHouse 4/11/2012

ISBN: 978-1-4685-8543-8 (e)
ISBN: 978-1-4685-8544-5 (hc)
ISBN: 978-1-4685-8545-2 (sc)

Library of Congress Control Number: 2012906500

Dedication

I dedicate this book of poems to my boyfriend Jeremy Earp (Frog). Who is the love of my life, my best friend, my inspiration and so much more. He has inspired me to write like never before. I am proud of you and proud to be a firefighter's girl! I love you for who you are and I always will! I love you with all my heart forever and always!

Contents

A Hero

You always held your head up high
Because you were proud of whom you were
You always believed in people
No matter whom they are
I went to see you
But I wish I could see you in person
You were always brave
Even though things would get difficult
Even though I want to be with you
I know I have to wait even though it's hard
I know I shouldn't ask why
But it's so hard not to know the reason why
My mind is always thinking of you
And I will never forget you
Even though I had to let you go
You will always be a part of me
I know you are following orders
But even though you're in heaven I will always love you
I guess heaven was
Needing a hero like you

A Little Child

Is a small and fragile
Because that's how God made them
Is so dear and precious
Because each one is unique in their own way
Is so sweet and joyful
Because they bring happiness to a home
Is dependent on people
Because they need someone they can count on
Is so very loved
Because they love you back

A Loved One

Is someone who patiently waits
To receive a letter from the one they love
Is someone who quickly opens the letter
To see what they wrote
Is someone who writes them almost every day
To tell them about the different things going on
Is someone who reads letters over and over again
Until the next one comes
Is someone who writes
To the one they hope to see again
Is someone who dreams
To hold their special someone in their arms again
Is someone who wants
To tell their true love that they will love them forever and always

A Mother

A mother is someone who loves you before you're born. She kisses you and gives you a hug before you go to bed at night. She is the one that holds you close to her at night when you cry. She is there to dry your tears and to comfort you in your time of need. She helps you through good and bad times. She teaches you certain things like how to cook, clean a house, and do laundry.

She watches you grow up from her little one, to a teenager, and then to an adult. When you turn thirteen, she hopes that you will take your teenage years slow because you can't go back in time and become younger. Then she watches you turn sixteen with worry because you're old enough to get your license. Finally, she watches you turn eighteen, graduate from high school and onto college in the fall. When you leave, she hugs you like the first day at the hospital when the doctors handed you to her.

When she gets a phone call with you telling her that you met someone and your relationship is getting serious. She tells you to pray and if that person is the one that you're supposed to be with then God will show you. She watches you while you're with that special person you brought home to meet the family. On that special day, she can't believe her "little girl" is standing before a preacher, saying her vow to the special man God has given her.

As time goes by, she watches you become a mother just like her. She watches you with your own baby and can't believe that you were once that little. She sees how happy you are with your new family and tells you how proud she is to be your mother. A mother is someone who will always love you and care for you in a special way.

A Rose with Thorns

A rose with thorns
Looks beautiful on the outside but is hard on the inside
A rose with thorns
Will prick you if you try to touch it
A rose with thorns
Will guard it from being hurt
A rose with thorns
Always does its best to try and defend itself
A rose with thorns
Wants someone that will protect it from harm
A rose with thorns
Looks for someone that will treat it with respect
A rose with thorns
Wants to have someone to trust
A rose with thorns
Wants someone that will always be there for them no matter what
A rose with thorns
Doesn't want thorns for the rest of its life
A rose with thorns
Wants to have a special someone that will help get rid of the thorns
A rose with thorns
Wants someone to love all of their days
A rose with thorns
Wants someone to love it back all of their days

A True Love

A true love
Is someone you can trust
A true love
Is someone that will support you in life
A true love
Is someone that God brings to you when the time is right
A true love
Is someone that will be next to you for life
A true love
Is someone that comes around once in a life time
A true love
Is someone that you love with all your heart
A true love
Is someone that will be there till death do you part

A Volunteer

A volunteer
Will go without being asked
A volunteer
Will go because they feel it's their duty
A volunteer
Will know the risks
A volunteer
Will make the sacrifices
A volunteer
Will go because they love their country
A volunteer
Will fight to keep their loved ones free
A volunteer
Will do their best
A volunteer
Will give their life

Abuse

Is critical
And will leave a trail of pieces
It can ruin a person's life
If they allow it to
It produces a lot of emotions
Sometimes to many to handle
They become distant
And they feel like they can't trust anyone
They try to cry for help
But something or someone stops them
They get angry easily
Because they are holding it all in
They try to tell someone
But not always in words
They feel damaged and useless
Because of what happened to them
They feel like it's them against the world
Because they feel so alone
They have been abused
In a way only certain people know what they are going through
Their life has been shattered
Because of someone else's actions
Happens to mostly children
Because they have a harder time defending themselves
It happens too much
And needs to be stopped

Always with You

In your mind
Because I will always be thinking of you
In your memory
Because we always had good times together
When you talked
Because I always gave anything to hear your voice
In your smile
Because I love seeing your smile
In your laugh
Because I enjoyed listening to you laugh
In your eyes
Because I always love looking into your eyes
When you sleep
Because watching you sleep peacefully makes me smile
When you're alone
Because I will never leave you
In your heart
Because I love you
When you love
Because I love the way you love me

Amazed

The way you look at me
With your soft blue eyes
The way you touch me
With your smooth finger s
The way you speak to me
With your sweet voice
The way you snuggle up with me
With a blanket over us and you holding me
The way you hold me
With your strong and calm arms
The way your there for me
With encouragement and love
The way you hold my hand
With gentleness
The way you kiss me
With your soft and smooth lips
The way you love me
With your heart of gold

America

America the land of the beautiful
But we have forgotten the real beauty of it
America is known as a godly nation
But we don't live like it
America has always been a free nation
But we take it for granted
America has been so blest by God
But we have forgotten that God gave us this nation
America is a republic
But people today are saying she is a democracy
America is slipping through the cracks
But are you trying to help save her or are you just letting her go

As Long As I Live

As long as I live
I will hold your hand till the earth stops spinning
As long as I live
I will keep my arms around you
As long as I live
I will stand next to you through the good and the bad times
As long as I live
I will always support you
As long as I live
I will never leave your side
As long as I live
You will be my prince charming
As long as I live
I will tell you I love you forever
As long as I live
I will love you till the day I take my last breath

Before You

Before you
I felt lost
Before you
I was afraid to trust people
Before you
I worried about letting people in my life
Before you
I didn't think anyone special would come into my life
Before you
I was happy but not as happy as I am now
Before you
I smiled and laughed but now it's all the time
Before you
I dreamed of falling in love with someone special and that person
turned out to be you

Being Close

When were close
We can play thumb wars
When were close
We both are safe
When were close
We can snuggle
When were close
We can have each other's arms wrapped around one another
When were close
We can have our heads on top of each other
When were close
We can feel each other's touch
When were close
We can feel each other's heartbeat

Belong

I belong with the one
Whose hand fits in mine
I belong with the one
Whose arms protect me
I belong with the one
Whose touch is tender
I belong with the one
Whose smile I can't forget
I belong with the one
Whose eyes I can't turn away from
I belong with the one
Whose voice I keep hearing
I belong with the one
Whose face I can't stop thinking about
I belong with the one
Whose love I can't let go of
I belong with the one
Who's going to help me raise our family
I belong with the one
Who's going to grow old with me
I belong with the one
Whose heart is always with me

Broken Road

The broken road
Is full of good and bad times
The broken road
Is full of broken dreams
The broken road
Is full of people that come and go
The broken road
Is full of happy and sad times
The broken road
Is a road that God can help you and lead you to the one he has for you

Courting

Courting
Is when we can't wait to see each other
Courting
Is when we can't wait to talk to each other
Courting
Is when we can't wait to spend time together
Courting
Is when we can call or write letters to each other
Courting
Is about learning how much a person means to you
Courting
Is learning how to be apart from each other
Courting
Is remembering that God is in it all until the end
Courting
Is learning to rely on God

Cross My Heart

I cross my heart
And I know I'll always get lost in your eyes
I cross my heart
And I'm happy I get to see your smile
I cross my heart
And I know we'll always be hand in hand
I cross my heart
And I always want to share our laughter together
I cross my heart
And I can't wait to share all of our joys
I cross my heart
And I'm so glad you're my dream come true
I cross my heart
And you will have my heart forever
I cross my heart
And I always want to be by your side
I cross my heart
And I'm glad we are each other's forever
I cross my heart
And I give you all of me

Cry

When you cried
I wrapped my arms around you
When you cried
I wanted to make you feel better
When you cried
I held you close to me to comfort you
When you cried
I talked to you so you knew you weren't alone
When you cried
I saw how sensitive and caring you were
When you cried
I dried your tears
When you cried
I stayed next to you because you mean so much to me
When you cried
I cried with you because I love you so very much

Do I

Do I love you right?

Because I want to show you different kinds of love

Do I love you right?

Because I want to show the best kind of love

Do I love you right?

Because I want to keep your love close

Do I love you right?

Because I want our love to be so strong

Do I love you right?

Because you're the love I always dreamed of

Do I love you right?

Because I want to love you right

Do I love you right?

Because I want to show you all the love I have for you

Do I love you right?

Because I won't ever stop loving you

Do I love you right?

Because I don't want you to ever think that I don't love you

Don't Take the Guy

Don't take the guy

Because I want to talk to him always

Don't take the guy

Because I want to always hear his voice

Don't take the guy

Because I want to see him smile everyday

Don't take the guy

Because I will miss him everyday

Don't take the guy

Because I love him

Don't take the guy

Because he completes me

Don't take the guy

Because I want him to see our kids grow up

Don't take the guy

Because he is my true love

Dreamed

I dreamed of us
Hold each other's hands forever
I dreamed of us
With our arms wrapped around each other
I dreamed of us
One day standing before a preacher
I dreamed of us
Being there through the good and bad times
I dreamed of us
Starting our own family together
I dreamed of us
Spending the rest of our lives together
I dreamed of us
Growing old until the day we took our last breath

Falling In Love

Falling in love
Is like wishing on a shooting star and it comes true
Falling in love
Is like a fairy tale but in real life
Falling in love
Is so amazing you can't even begin to imagine
Falling in love
Is something I never thought would ever happen to me
Falling in love
Is when you get butterflies in your stomach and they stay there
Falling in love
Is when your heart hurts and longs to be with the one you love
Falling in love
Is when you can't stop thinking and don't want to stop thinking of that
special person

Family

A family is

A group of people who care about you

A family is

A group of people who care what you do with your life and future

A family is

A group of people who will be there through trials

A family is

A group of people who will pray for you day and night

A family is

A group of people who love each other through thick and thin

A family is

A group of people who make it worth coming home

A family is

Something I have, won't let it go, or forget it

Firefighters

Firefighters are a group of people
Who make sacrifices all the time
Firefighters are a group of people
Who are there when we need them
Firefighters are a group of people
Who are on call day and night
Firefighters are a group of people
Who put their life on the line every day
Firefighters are a group of people
Who need to be thanked every day for being there for us
Firefighters are a group of people
Who need our prayers every day
Firefighters are a group of people
Who need our support
Firefighters are a group of brave men and women
Who are greatly appreciated for everything they have done

Firefighters 2

Firefighter's respond to many different kinds of calls
Because that's part of their job
Firefighter's are there for you all day long
Because they care about people
Firefighter's rescue so many people
Because they care and don't want anything to happen to them
Firefighter's families and loved ones pray every day for them
Because they want them to stay safe and come home at the end of the day
Firefighter's make a lot of sacrifices
Because being a firefighter means so much to them
Firefighter's pray that they will make it through
Because they want to keep living so they can help more people
Firefighter's risk their own lives
Because they are there to help save lives of others
Firefighter's fall on their knees to thank God
Because they made it through a blazing fire
Firefighter's are always there
Because they signed up for being there for people
Firefighters should always be appreciated
Because those of us who aren't one don't know what it really takes to be one
Firefighter's sometimes die
But we need to make sure we're there for their families since they were there for us
Firefighters are proud of what they do
Because they enjoy helping their community

Forever & Always

I want to keep my hand in yours forever and always
Because your hand is the only one that mine fits in
I want to hold you for forever and always
Because you're the only one I want to wrap my arms around
I want to there for you forever and always
Because you are there for me
I want to be married to you forever and always
Because you are my one and only true love
I want to kiss you forever and always
Because you're the only one I want to give my kisses to
I want to open my eyes and see you forever and always
Because you're the only one I want to wake up next to
I want to be the mother of your kids forever and always
Because you're the only one I want a family with
I will love you forever and always
Because you're the one I will love till the moment I take my last breath

Frog

You're my man
Because you're my knight in shining armor
You're my best friend
And I would give my life to save you
You have the most wonderful laugh
And can make me laugh like no one else
You have the most amazing smile
Your forever warms my soul
When I look in your eyes
Always seem to get lost in them
Hearing your voice
Makes my heart melt
Your hugs
Keep me safe from harm
Your kisses
Is something that I don't want to end
When I look at your butt
I always knew it was really cute
When you run your fingers through
I feel the tenderness of your fingertips
Your hands are so soft and gentle
And your touch is so warm
When you hold me tight
I get to be so close to you
Your heart is amazing
I can see inside it and it's so kind and caring
I want us to make many memories
And always laugh and smile
When I need someone to count on
I know we can always count on each other

I trust you with all my heart
And I know we'll always be there for each other
You're my lover
And my one and only true love
I love you so very much my love
And I will love you forever and always
Tippy loves Frog
Tippy and Frog forever

From This Moment

You have my hands
To keep you close
You have my hugs
To keep you safe
You have my eyes
Because I love looking at you
You have my kisses
Because I love touching your lips with mine
You have my love
Because I trust you
You have my heart
Because you're my best friend
You have all of me
Because you are forever my guy

Give Me That Guy

That wants to cuddle
When watching a movie
That wants to spend time together
Whenever there is time
That wants to share his love
With someone he wants forever
That wants to start a family
With the one he loves
That wants only one love
Because that's the guy I want for eternity
That wants to grow old
With his love sitting in the chair next to him
That wants to share his life
With someone who is special to him

Give

I give you
My smile and laughter
I give you
My hands and arms
I give you
My hugs and kisses
I give you
My heart for life
I give you
My hand for marriage
I give you
My "I love you"

God Knew

I needed someone I could laugh with
Because laughter is good for you
I needed someone I could run to
Because we all need someone to be there for us
I needed someone to hold
Because people need to be able to cuddle with the one they love
I needed someone I could share things with
Because communication is the key to a relationship
I needed someone to cherish
Because love is always important
I needed someone special
So he gave me you
I needed someone I could love without any doubts
Because that means you can love them unconditionally

God's Timing

Is perfect for us
Because it will be in his timing
Is good for us
Because it will test us
Is something to want
Because it's what God wants
Is something to pray for
Because it will help us trust in him
Is showing us different things
Because we are waiting on him
Is always wonderful
Because he will never fail us

Good Morning

How was your night?

It was perfect because we were holding each other

How was your night?

It was perfect because we were together

How was your night?

It was perfect because I got to watch you sleep peacefully

How was your night?

It was perfect because I got to look into your eyes

How was your night?

It was perfect because I got to kiss you

How was your night?

It was perfect because I got to tell you that I love you

How was your night?

It was perfect because I was next to the one I love

How was your night?

It was perfect because I got to wake up next to the one I get to grow old with

How was your night?

It was perfect because you're the one I get to spend the rest of my life with

Guess What (Her)

Guess what

You're the one I always want to hold hands with

Guess what

I can't wait to hold you in my arms forever

Guess what

You are the one who brings joy and happiness to my life

Guess what

You are my best friend and will be forever

Guess what

You are my princess

Guess what

You are my one and only true love forever and always

Guess what

We will always be together no matter what

Guess what

I love you with all my heart and I will never stop loving you

Guess what

As your walking down the aisle towards me I see the love of my life

Guess what

We will spend our lives together till our last breath on earth

Guess What II (Her)

You're the one I always want to hold hands with
Because your hand matches mine
I can't wait to hold you in my arms forever
Because you're the only woman I love holding
You are the one who brings joy and happiness to my life
Because you helped me with so much
You are my best friend and will be forever
Because you are my one and only girl
You are my princess
Because you are the girl I care about
You are my one and only true love forever and always
Because you are the only one I want
We will always be together no matter what
Because we are destined to be with one another
I love you with all my heart and I will never stop loving you
Because you mean everything to me
As your walking down the aisle towards me I see the love of my life
Because you're the girl I can't wait to be with forever
We will spend our lives together till our last breath on earth
Because we want to always be together

Guess What (Him)

Guess what
You're the one I want to hold hands with
Guess what
You're the one I want to hold forever
Guess what
You are my best friend and you always will be
Guess what
You are my knight in shining armor
Guess what
You are my one and only true love
Guess what
We will always be together
Guess what
I love you with all my heart and I always will
Guess what
When I walk down the aisle I will be walking towards the man I love
Guess what
We get to spend our lives together forever

Guess What II (Him)

You're the one I want to hold hands with
Because our hands fit in each other's perfectly
You're the one I want to hold forever
Because you are the only man I imagine my arms around
You are my best friend and you always will be
Because you are my other half
You are my knight in shining armor
Because you are always there to rescue me
You are my one and only true love
Because you are the man that completes me
We will always be together
Because you're the man God blest me with
I love you with all my heart and I always will
Because you are everything and more to me
When I walk down the aisle I will be walking towards the man I love
Because you're the one I am meant to be with
We get to spend our lives together forever
Because we don't want it any other way

Happy Anniversary

Happy anniversary

To the man I started a new life with

Happy anniversary

To the man I get to see everyday

Happy anniversary

To the man that makes me happier than anyone else

Happy anniversary

To the man I gave my whole heart to

Happy anniversary

To the man I get to share this special day with every month

Happy anniversary

To the man I get to spend till the end of time with

Happy anniversary

To the man I will be next to for the rest of our lives

Happy Birthday

To the one
I hold close to me
To the one
I get to watch blow out candles
To the one
I want to make smile on this special day
To the one
I get to spend this special day with
To the one
 I will be there for on this day
To the one
I get to grow old with
To the one
I will give a gift to from my heart
To the one
I will always keep in my heart

Hope

I hope

My soldier's prayers reach heaven

I hope

My soldier knows they are greatly missed

I hope

My soldier stays safe

I hope

My soldier knows I'm always thinking of them

I hope

My soldier knows their courage helps keep them strong

I hope

My soldier knows they are loved

I hope

My soldier gets to dream again

I hope

My soldier gets to come back home

I hope

My soldier looks at the stars at night and thinks of us

I hope

My soldier knows how proud I am of them

I hope

My soldier knows I will always be waiting here

I hope

My soldier knows my heart will always be with them

I hope

My soldier knows that they will always have my love

How Do I

How do I
Talk to you since you're not here
How do I
Not get upset
How do I
Go to sleep with you gone
How do I
Keep the nightmares away
How do I
Wake up every morning without you
How do I
Keep from crying myself to sleep every night
How do I
Not forget my best friend
How do I
Breathe when you're not here
How do I
Keep going on without you
How do I
Keep living my life
How do I
Respond when the one I love took their last breath

Hug & Kisses

My hugs and kisses
Are for the one who brings joy and happiness to my life
My hugs and kisses
Are for the man I will give my heart to
My hugs and kisses
Are for the only one I love
My hugs and kisses
Are for the one I will spend forever with
My hugs and kisses
Are only for my husband
My hugs and kisses
Are for the man I want to have a family with
My hugs and kisses
Are for the one I can't live without

I Believe 1

I believe

Our lives are starting a new path

I believe

Our love is true and that we were brought together by God

I believe

Our kind of love is one of the best

I believe

Our love shows on the outside and others like seeing couples in love

I believe

Our relationship is based on trust

I believe

Our love is a bond of friendship

I believe

That despite what some people say we will make it

I believe

Our love is the kind of love others want

I believe

Our love is so strong only God could separate us

I Believe 2

Our lives are starting a new path
Because we've made a commitment to one another
Our love is true and that we were brought together by God
Because no one else knew that we would be perfect for one another
Our kind of love is one of the best
Because God is in it
Our love shows on the outside and others like seeing couples in love
Because it's something they have with the one they love
Our relationship is based on trust
Because without it there is no real love
Our love is a bond of friendship
Because it helps our love to grow stronger
That despite what some people say we will make it
Because we are two pieces of a puzzle that make a whole
Our love is the kind of love others want
Because it's unconditional and endless
Our love is so strong only God could separate us
Because he is the only one strong enough to do it

I Can't Believe

I can't believe
That we have so much in common
I can't believe
That we get to talk everyday
I can't believe
That we get to make memories together
I can't believe
That we get to see each other everyday
I can't believe
That we get to hold hands forever
I can't believe
That we get to share what God has for both of us
I can't believe
That we finally found each other
I can't believe
That we get to wake up next to each other
I can't believe
That we get to tell each other "I love you" everyday
I can't believe
That we get to start our own family together
I can't believe
That we get to spend the rest of our lives together

I Love You

I love you
Because your you
I love you
Because you love God
I love you
Because you're my best friend
I love you
Because God brought us together
I love you
Because you're my knight in shining armor
I love you
Because I get to share my life with you
I love you
Because you're the love of my life

I Need

Someone I can hold

Because I want to be close to him

Someone I can take care of

Because I want him to know he means the world to me

Someone I can be there for

Because I want to show him the love I have for him

Someone I can talk to about anything

Because I want him to talk to me about anything

Someone I can trust

Because he's the one I want to always be with

Someone I can wake up next to every morning

Because he's the first one I want to see when I open my eyes

Someone I can go to sleep with every night

Because he's the last person I want to see before I close my eyes

Someone I can wrap my arms around

Because I will never let go of him

Someone special

Because he is the beat to my heart

My one and only true love

Because I can't live without him

Someone I can love with all of my heart

Because he's the one I will spend the rest of my life with

My prince

Because you complete me

My babe

Because you're the one I love so much

Frog I need you

Because you're the one I will love till the day I take my last breath

I Pray

That I get to hold hands
With you all of our days
That I get to hold you
Till the end of time
That I get to say goodnight to you
Because you're the one I want to see before I close my eyes
That I get to any good morning to you
Because you're the first one I want to see when I wake up
That I get to watch you with our kids
Because I know you will make the best dad
That I get to love you
For a lifetime

I Think

Of us all day
When I'm working
Of us all night
When I'm dreaming
Of us holding each other
When we are going through good and bad times
Of us loving each other everyday
Because I want to love you forever
Of us spending forever and always together
Because you are my one and only true love
Of us having a family together
Because I want us to have kids
Of us growing old together
Because I want to be with you till I take my last breath

I Want

To be there when you aren't feeling good
Because I want to be the one to take care of you
To be there for you
Because I don't want you to hurt ever again
Us to be happy together
Because we are perfect together
To be with you so bad
Because I love you so much
Our love to get stronger
Because I never want it to break
You to be here beside me
Because you are my best friend
Us to be together
Because I know that you are my true love
Love you with all my heart
Because I want to marry you
You to be the one I have a family with
Because I want us to become parents
You in my life
Because I want to spend the rest of our lives together
You next to me forever
Because I want to hold you and kiss you anytime I want

I Would Do Anything

I would do anything for you
Because you're my everything
I would do anything for you
Because you're my best friend for life
I would do anything for you
Because you're the guy I have always dreamed of
I would do anything for you
Because you're the one I think about all the time
I would do anything for you
Because you're the one I want to have a life with
I would do anything for you
Because you're the only one for me
I would do anything for you
Because you're the one I would lay down my life for
I would do anything for you
Because you're my true love
I would do anything for you
Because the one that was given to me by God
I would do anything for you
Because you're the one I can't live without
I would do anything for you
Because you're the one I get to spend my life with

If I Lost You

If I lost you
I wouldn't be able to hold you
If I lost you
I wouldn't be able to comfort you
If I lost you
I wouldn't be able to hold your hand
If I lost you
I wouldn't be able to hug you everyday
If I lost you
I wouldn't be able to look into your eyes
If I lost you
I wouldn't get to hear your voice everyday
If I lost you
I wouldn't be able to see your wonderful smile
If I lost you
I wouldn't be able to hear your great laugh
If I lost you
I will have lost my best friend
If I lost you
I wouldn't be able to wake up with you next to me
If I lost you
I wouldn't be able to kiss you
If I lost you
I wouldn't be able to tell you how much I miss you
If I lost you
I wouldn't be able to tell you that you will always be in my heart
If I lost you
I wouldn't be able to tell you how much you mean to me

If I lost you

I wouldn't be able to tell you how much I love you

If I lost you

I will have lost my true love

If you're Reading This

If you're reading this
Remember that I will always love you
If you're reading this
Remember that I fought for you and my country
If you're reading this
I won't be able to be by your side
If you're reading this
I will miss you
If you're reading this
I served my country to help keep her free
If you're reading this
I know you prayed for me everyday
If you're reading this
I didn't make it
If you're reading this
God called me home
If you're reading this
I know you loved me with all your heart
If you're reading this
I want you to know I'll always love you

I'll Be There 1

I'll be there
When you want to talk
I'll be there
When you want a shoulder to cry on
I'll be there
When you need to be held
I'll be there
When you need someone to dry your tears
I'll be there
When you need a best friend
I'll be there
When you need anything
I'll be there
When you need to be loved

I'll Be There 2

When you need someone to talk to
I will listen
When you need someone to listen to your heart
I will be next to you
When you need someone to hold you
I will wrap my arms around you
When you need someone to cry with
I will show you compassion
When you need someone to help you
I will be there
When you need someone to comfort you
I will be waiting here
When you need someone to love
I will love you with all my heart

I'm Sorry Baby

I'm sorry baby
I thought I was doing the right thing
I'm sorry baby
I didn't mean for this to happen
I'm sorry baby
I should have told the doctor "No"
I'm sorry baby
I didn't include you and God in my decision
I'm sorry baby
It's something I will always regret for the rest of my life

Imagine

I try to imagine
Every hair on your head
I try to imagine
The color of your eyes
I try to imagine
The gentleness and kindness in your eyes
I try to imagine
Your wonderful smile
I try to imagine
Your voice and laugh
I try to imagine
All these put together and I imagine the best person in my life

I'm Already There

I'm already there
When you hear the kids laughing
I'm already there
When you see the kids smile
I'm already there
When you see them playing
I'm already there
When you feel the wind blowing
I'm already there
When you are happy and sad
I'm already there
When you think of us
I'm already there
When you cry tears of joy and sadness
I'm already there
When you lay awake at night
I'm already there
When you look at the ring on your hand
I'm already there
When you go through trials and hardships
I'm already there
When I'm in your heart
I'm already there
And I will never leave you

I'm Already There 2

When you hear the kids laughing
I am laughing with them
When you see the kids smile
I am right there smiling with them
When you see them playing
I am their imaginary friend
When you feel the wind blowing
I am talking to you
When you are happy and sad
I am there to cheer and comfort you
When you think of us
I am right there sitting next to you
When you cry tears of joy and sadness
I am here to wipe them
When you lay awake at night
I am right there beside you
When you look at the ring on your hand
I'm already there
When you go through trials and hardships
I am already holding it in mine
When I'm in your heart
I am already praying to God to help you through
I will never leave you
Because God brought us together forever

I'll be

I'll be the one
You can count on
I'll be the one
You can talk to about anything
I'll be the one
Who will give you a shoulder to cry on
I'll be the one
To comfort you
I'll be the one
Who will take care of you
I'll be the one
To hold you close and tight
I'll be the one
Who will help you when you fall
I'll be the one
Who will never leave you
I'll be the one
Who will stand next to you no matter what
I'll be the one
To love you unconditionally

In the Night

We hold each other close
Because we love being so close to one another
Our legs are tangled together
Because we love the feel of them together
I stroke my fingers across your face
Because I love watching you as you close your eyes
You run your fingers through my hair
Because you enjoy feeling how soft it is
We kiss
Because we want it to be the last thing we do before closing our eyes
We say "I love you"
Because we want each other to know how much we mean to each other
We say "Good-night"
Because we want each other to have sweet dreams

In Your Eyes

In your eyes
I know how much you care for me
In your eyes
I know how much you love me
In your eyes
I know you'll never let go
In your eyes
I know that you will always be there
In your eyes
I know we'll always be together
In your eyes
I know I could look in them forever
In your eyes
I know that God gave you to me

Independence Day

Is a day when we honor
The men and women who have served
Is a day when we honor
The men and women who gave their lives
Is a day when we honor
Our nation that God gave us
Is a day when we honor
The men and women who are still serving
Is a day when we honor
All the branches of our military
Is a day when we honor
The flag of our country
Is a day when we remember
That we still have a free nation

Is It Love

Is it love?
When I get excited about seeing you
Is it love?
When I hear your name and blush
Is it love?
When I see you and can't stop smiling
Is it love?
When I talk to you and my mind goes blank
Is it love?
When I hear your voice and melt
Is it love?
When I want to be around you all the time
Is it love?
When I can't wait for you to smile
Is it love?
When I want to hear you laugh
Is it love?
When I think about you all of the time
Is it love?
When I can't imagine my life without you
Is it love?
When I want to love you forever

Little Moments

Little moments
Create new memories
Little moments
Will come at anytime
Little moments
Can cause laughter
Little moments
Can cause tears
Little moments
Can show imperfection
Little moments
Can change things
Little moments
Can cause us to lose track of time
Little moments
Will always happen in life
Little moments
Will always be remembered
Little moments
Can show your love
Little moments
Should be cherished

Love Letters

Love Letters
Are for the one that you want to see every morning when you wake up
Love Letters
Are for the one that you want to see every night when you go to sleep
Love Letters
Are for the one that you want to hold onto forever
Love Letters
Are for the one who you can't imagine life without
Love Letters
Are for the one who you want to be by your side forever
Love Letters
Are for the one you love with all your heart

Love

Is something beautiful
Because it's from God
Is something you cherish
Because it's a gift
Is something that is sacred
Because it's a treasure
Is something that is very real
Because of the way we show it
Is something I have for you
Because you mean everything to me
Is from my heart to yours
Because you are my special someone

Meant To Be

We are meant to be together

Because we want to always hold each other

We are meant to be together

Because we don't want to stop thinking of each other

We are meant to be together

Because God has brought us together

We are meant to be together

Because you are my true love and I am your true love

We are meant to be together

Because we love each other with all of our hearts

We are meant to be together

Because we can't imagine our life without one another

We are meant to be together

Because we want to start a new life together

We are meant to be together

Because we will love each other till the day we die

Memories

Memories
Are made with the one you love
Memories
Are made of good and bad times
Memories
Are made of smiles and laughter
Memories
Are made of tears of joy and sorrow
Memories
Is something you won't forget
Memories
Is something you can always take with you
Memories
Is something we can always cherish
Memories
Is something I want to share with our family
Memories
Is something I don't want to stop making
Memories
Is something I want to create with you

Miscarriage

Is like a nightmare
And you hope when you wake up it didn't really happen
Is so hard to go through
Because that was your baby
Makes you question what happened
Because you don't understand
Makes you cry so hard and so long
But you eventually lose the strength to cry anymore
Makes you wonder what they would have looked like
But you already know they would have looked beautiful
Makes you wonder who they would have turned out to be
But you already know that they would have turned out to be wonderful
Makes you glad that they're in heaven
Because they are safe, healthy, and with God

Mom

You found out you were pregnant
But yet you didn't want me
You say it was all a mistake
But yet you allow them to take my life
You say you're doing what's best for me
But yet you don't consider the plans that God night have for me
You say it's hard to be a mother
But yet all I want is a mother to love me
You say this is for the better
But yet I feel I'm being punished
You say you don't want a child yet
But yet I don't even get a chance to be adopted
You say that this is the only way
But yet I'm just a baby that wants to be loved and cared for
God designed every baby. He makes them different and unique in their own way. He sends them here for us to look after, but instead we kill them before they get a chance at life outside of the womb.
Babies also have a right to life because they are human just like us. Even if we ourselves can't take care of them, we at least need to give them to someone who will take good care of them.

My Arms

Are here to hold you
When you need someone to be close to you
Are here to comfort you
When you need someone to be there for you
Are here for you every time
When you have nowhere to turn
Are here to keep you from harm
When you need to feel safe
Are here to love you
When you want someone to love you
Are here forever
And will never close

My Belly

Is getting big
Because there is a little one growing inside me
Is stretching
Because my baby is stretching
Will move
When the baby kicks
Is hard
And it keeps my little one safe
Will carry my baby
For about nine months
Is carrying something very special
And will always be special

My Best Friend

My best friend
Is someone I want to talk to about anything
My best friend
Is someone I want to be next to through thick and thin
My best friend
Is someone I want to hold and comfort
My best friend
Is someone I want to laugh and smile with
My best friend
Is someone I want to hold hands with
My best friend
Is someone I want to be there for
My best friend
Is someone I want to pray with everyday
My best friend
Is someone I want to watch grow in the Lord
My best friend
Is someone I want to share my life with
My best friend
Is someone I want to have a family with
My best friend
Is someone I want to grow old with
My best friend
Is someone I want to share my heart with forever

My Every Thing

You're my every thing
Because you're my true love
You're my every thing
Because you complete me
You're my every thing
Because we dry one another's tears
You're my every thing
Because we hold each other when we need to be comforted
You're my every thing
Because if one of us loses pieces the other one helps pick them up
You're my every thing
Because if one heart is breaking the other one helps keep it together
You're my every thing
Because you're the only one I will ever love
You're my every thing
Because I will always be there for you

My First

You were my first
Boyfriend to cuddle and hold me close
You were my first
Boyfriend to hug me and have it forever
You were my first
Boyfriend to touch me with gentle hands
You were my first
Boyfriend to run your fingers through my hair
You were my first
Kiss and you will be my last
You were my first
Lover and it will always be only you
You were my first
Boyfriend and one day we'll become one

My Heart

My heart
Fills up with joy
My heart
Is sad when were apart
My heart
Gets so excited
My heart
Feels like it wants to jump
My heart
Beats so fast when I'm with you
My heart
Loves you and only you

My Love

You don't have to say a word
Because I know what you're thinking
You don't have to ask
Because I already have the answer
You don't have to wonder
Because I will always be there for you
You don't have to cry
Because I will never leave you
You don't have to be sad
Because my hand will always be in yours
You don't have to dream
Because you already have my heart
You don't have to be worried
Because I will love you forever and always
You don't have to be scared
Because you're my one and only true love

My Man

My man holds me close and tight
Because he'll never let go
My man kisses me with passion
Because I am the only one he wants
My man tells me he loves me
Because he'll always be there for me
My man tells me one day we'll be together
Because I am his true love
My man promises me he will love me till the day he dies
Because I am the only one he wants to love till his last day

My Marine

My marine is courageous
Because he is willing to go to war
My marine is brave
Because he is willing to die for the ones he loves
My marine is honored
Because of the sacrifices he has made
My marine is supported
Because he means everything to me
My marine is always being prayed for
Because his loved ones want him to be safe
My marine is thought about everyday
Because he is loved and missed by the ones who love him
My marine is loved every second of the day
Because he is my best friend and my hero

I love my marine with all my heart and I will always will. He is the only one I will ever truly love. I will be right here waiting for him when he comes home with my arms wide open.

My Mind

Can't think right
Because you're always on my mind
Goes blank
Because your voice is the only thing I hear
Loves thinking of you
Because you mean so much to me
Can't stop thinking of you
Because you're my special guy
Doesn't want to stop thinking of you
Because you're the one I love to think about

My Valentine

My valentine and I
Get to hold one another
My valentine and I
Get to make new memories
My valentine and I
Get to share happiness
My valentine and I
Get to have our first valentine's day together
My valentine and I
Get to spend a special day together
My valentine and I
Get to give each other special gifts
My valentine and I
Get to show our love for each other
My valentine and I
Get to spend time just you and me

Never Saw

Such a gentleness and kindness
From a guy that is so sweet
A smile and laugh
That is so wonderful to see and listen to
Such amazing eyes
That is so caring and understanding
Things in a different light
Until you came along
Such a big heart
Who is willing to help anyone
The kind of love you show me
From someone who cares for me so much
Such a handsome guy
With so much love

Never Thought

I never thought
That my dreams would come true
I never thought
That I would ever trust anyone as much as I trust you
I never thought
That I would ever fall in love
I never thought
That the greatest guy ever would love me
I never thought
That love would feel like this
I never thought
That I would ever feel this way about anyone
I never thought
That I would love someone as much as I love you
I never thought
But now I know you are my one true love

Nine Months

For nine months
I get to feel you move
For nine months
I get to feel you grow
For nine months
I get to pray for you everyday
For nine months
I get to see you in my belly
For nine months
I get to hear your heart beat
For nine months
I get to carry you in my belly

No One

Sees me

Because I'm invisible to them

Gives me a chance

Because they think they already know me

Understands me

Because they don't take the time to try to get to know the real me

Wants to hear me

Because someone else told them different

Wants me around

Because they want me to change

Wants me to talk to them

Because I don't do what they want

Only Love

Only love
Is going to be sad and happy
Only love
Is going to be free and real
Only love
Is going to be so amazing and beyond our imagination
Only love
Is going to be like a dream come true
Only love
Is going to be unbreakable and true
Only love
Is going to be enough because our hearts fit together
Only love
Is going to last for ever

Only You & God

Can hold me
Because I know neither of you would never let me go
Can make me feel this way
Because both of you love me in a special way
Can fill the place in my heart
Because both of you complete me
Can love me as much as I love you
Because both of you are my true loves

Only You

Only you
Always believe in me
Only you
Always show me new things
Only you
Always helps bring peace to my heart
Only you
Always helps me figure things out
Only you
Always brings so much happiness to my life
Only you
Always helps me when no one else will
Only you
Always brings music to my heart
Only you
Always makes me laugh when I want to cry
Only you
Always stands by me whenever I need you

Only Yours

I'm only yours

Because you're the only one that makes my heart beat faster

I'm only yours

Because you're the only one that makes me get butterflies in my stomach

I'm only yours

Because you mean everything to me and you always will

I'm only yours

Because my hand fits perfectly in yours

I'm only yours

Because you're my prince charming

I'm only yours

Because you're the only one for me

I'm only yours

Because you're the one who holds the key to my heart

Our Four Fathers

Our four fathers
Fought for our country
Our four fathers
Fought for what they had come to love
Our four fathers
Fought for what they believed in
Our four fathers
Stood up for God
Our four fathers
Stood up for what was right
Our four fathers
Signed the declaration of Independence to help America
Our four fathers
What would they think about our country now?

Our Hearts

We are destined to be together
For a special reason
We are woven together
So we become one
We are designed a certain way
So that when you put them together you know they fit
We are meant to fall in love
Because God knew we needed each other
We are made for each other
Because God created them to fit together

Our Rings

Have special meanings to them
Because we know that we are meant to be together
Show our love for each other
As we stand before a preacher
Represents something special between us
Because we are giving ourselves to each other
Symbolizes that we belong to each other
Till death do us part
Are in the shape of a circle
Because our love for each other will never end

Perfect

Means life will be boring
Because there are things you can't learn
Means you can't learn from books or people
Because you already have all the knowledge
Means you can do no wrong
But then we can't learn from our mistakes
Means you don't need people to be there
Because you can do everything on your own
Means you don't need people to help you
But you miss out on family and friends working to help you
Means you don't need anyone special
Because you're already perfect

Plan On Forever

I can plan on forever with you

Because you are the answers to my prayers

I can plan on forever with you

Because all my dreams have come true

I can plan on forever with you

Because we are meant for one another

I can plan on forever with you

Because God brought us together

I can plan on forever with you

Because you're the only one I want

I can plan on forever with you

Because I know you'll be right there beside me till the end of time

Prayer of a Soldier

That their loved ones are safe
Because they mean so much to them
They get to see their loved ones again
Because they long to see them smiling at them
They get to talk to them again
Because they long to hear their loved ones say "I love you"
To get to hold them again
Because they long to keep them close to them
To do their best to defend their country
Because America is their home
That they get to live another day
Because they dream of their loved ones everyday
To be able to go home
Because they dream of living their life

Promise

I promise
To hold you through the good and the bad times
I promise
To be there for you no matter what
I promise
To keep only to you
I promise
To care for you till the day I die
I promise
To cherish you to the ends of the earth
I promise
To love you all the days of my life

Remember When

Remember when we first met
It was love at first sight
Remember when we first held hands
It was then we knew we would hold hands forever
Remember when we first told each other that we loved one another
It was then we knew we were meant to be together forever
Remember when you got down on one knee
It was the day I agreed to spend forever with you
Remember when we first held each other
It was then we would never let go of one another
Remember when we were married
It was then we would start our new life together
Remember when we first kissed
It was then we would always kiss each other
Remember when we said till death do us part
It's a promise that we both intend to keep forever

Smile

Seeing you smile
Makes me smile on the inside and outside
Seeing you smile
Brightens up my day
Seeing you smile
Makes me glad were together
Seeing you smile
Makes me so happy
Seeing you smile
Reminds me how lucky I am to have you
Seeing you smile
Makes my heart melt
Seeing you smile
Brings joy and laughter to my soul
Seeing you smile
Makes me love you even more
Seeing you smile
Makes me glad I get to see you every day for the rest of my life

Soldiers

You fight to keep our nation free
But we act like we don't want to be free
You fight to save other people's lives
But we act like we don't care if we live or die
You fight to help others
But we turn our backs on them
You fight for what is right
But we don't acknowledge it
You fight in a battle
Knowing that you may never come back
You fought in a war
Knowing that you gave your life for your family and country

Thank you soldiers for giving your lives to help save a stubborn nation like us. Over the years we have become an ungrateful nation. We need to remember the men and women who have dedicated and who have given their lives to serve our country and the people in it.

Still the One

You're still the one
That has my hand
You're still the one
That has my hugs
You're still the one
I can't wait to wake up next to you every morning
You're still the one
I can't wait to go to sleep next to you every night
You're still the one
I go to when I need to be held
You're still the one
I want to stand next to through good and bad times
You're still the one
That has my kisses
You're still the one
I hold in my heart
You're still the one
I love you so much
You're still the one
I want a family with
You're still the one
That has my heart
You're still the one
I will always love
You're still the one
I want to spend eternity with

Stone Angel

She learned

That she's all alone

She learned

That if you let someone in you get hurt

She learned

To stay away from everyone

She learned

That life is so hard even when you're a child

She learned

Not to let anyone touch you

She learned

To cave to fear

She learned

No one seems to care about what has happened to her

She learned

That people looked down on her because she was different

She learned

That she couldn't look at men in the eyes

She learned

That when she cried no one was there for her

She learned

That she was never really safe

She learned

That she felt used and abandoned

She learned

That she had no one she could trust

She learned

To push people out of her life

She learned

That no one knew the real her

She learned

That her heart had become hard like a stone

She learned

That she just wanted someone to treat her right

She learned

That she just wanted someone to hold her

She learned

That she wanted someone to protect her

She learned

That it's so hard to keep going

She learned

If she erased something from her mind it would be the memories of that week

She learned

That even though life is hard she shouldn't give up

Stone Angel 2

She felt all alone
But she realized there are others like her and that she's not alone
It felt like every time she let someone in, she got hurt
But then she realized she could be close to someone and not get hurt
She wouldn't let anyone touch her
But she found out someone's touch can be gentle, kind, and loving
Fear was one of the only things she knew
But she found she could overcome it
She didn't think anyone cared about her
But she noticed that some people do care about her
She didn't like it when people looked down on her
But she learned not to care what they thought
She was so afraid to look men in the eyes
But now she can look anyone in the eyes and stand her ground
She didn't think when she cried anyone could hear her
But God heard her and was always with her
She never felt safe
But she can defend herself now
She didn't have people she felt she could trust
But now she knows what it's like to trust someone
She knew how to push people away
But she found out she doesn't have to push people away to stay safe
Her heart had become stone
But she learned not to let her heart be so hard
She had felt abandoned and used
But she met someone who won't abandon or use her because he cares
for her
She didn't know how to love someone
But God brought someone along and showed her how to love
She just wanted to erase memories of her past

But she knew she couldn't so she learned to conquer them
She wanted to be an angel
But she found out she doesn't have to be an angel, just to find someone
who loves and respects you
She didn't think she could make it through
But she found out she can make it
She didn't think she'd ever be happy
But she found so much happiness and is full of life again
She didn't think God would love her anymore
But he loves her no matter what and always will

Surprise

Surprise my love
We get to learn new things along the way
Surprise my love
We get to share new memories
Surprise my love
We get to share our love
Surprise my love
We get to take care of a bundle of joy
Surprise my love
We have a little gift on its way
Surprise my love
You will soon be a daddy

Tears

Tears
Come with joy
Tears
Come when you have pain
Tears
Come when you lose someone
Tears
Come with sadness
Tears
Come at good and hard times
Tears
Come unexpectedly
Tears
Come like a stream
Tears
Come at special times
Tears
Come because you love someone so much

The Hope Chest

The hope chest
Holds many different things
The hope chest
Holds things from your past
The hope chest
Holds things for your future
The hope chest
Holds memories
The hope chest
Holds things that are special
The hope chest
Holds things that are precious
The hope chest
Comes in many sizes

The Love of a Child

The love of a child
Is very deep
The love of a child
Is sweet and dear
The love of a child
Is so very precious
The love of a child
Is something to cherish
The love of a child
Is something to hold onto forever

The One

You're the one
I get to share new things with
You're the one
I get to listen to as you tell stories
You're the one
I get to share memories with
You're the one
I get to always be with
You're the one
I get to hold until the end of time
You're the one
I get to see with our kids
You're the one
I get to share my heart with
You're the one
I get to sit next to in a rocking chair as we grow older
You're the one
I get live my life with

The Stars

As we sit under the stars
You hold my hand in yours
As we sit under the stars
You sit close enough so I can put my head on your shoulder
As we sit under the stars
We remember the first time we looked at the stars and thought of each
other
As we sit under the stars
We see a shooting star and make a wish
As we sit under the stars
We talk about our dreams
As we sit under the stars
We talk about the future
As we sit under the stars
We thank God that we are together
As we sit under the stars
We know that we get to do this forever

This Day

This is the day
This is the day I will walk down the aisle towards the man I love
This is the day
I will marry my best friend
This is the day
I will make a vow to him
This is the day
I will say "I do"
This is the day
I will give my heart to him
This is the day
I will never forget the look on his face
This is the day
I will become a wife
This is the day
I will forever and always be his

Together

We get to hold hands
Because our hands fit perfectly
We get to see each other face to face
Because we love looking in each other's eyes
We get to see each other smile
Because we always love seeing the other one smile
We get to hear each other's laugh
Because we have so much happiness and joy
We get to hold onto one another
Because we want the other one to know we will never let go
We get to whisper in each other's ear
Because we always tell each other "I love you"
We get to go do special things
Because we love spending time together
We get to go to special places
Because we love making new memories
We get to be side by side
Because we love being together
We get to snuggle
Because we want to be close to one another
We get to share special memories
Because we will get to cherish them
We get to wipe away one another's tears
Because we will always be there for each other
We get to show each other our love
Because we want to always show it
We have great love
Because we have strong love
We are the greatest couple
Because we are meant to be together forever

Traveling Soldier

The traveling soldier
Thinks of many things
The traveling soldier
Thinks of their loved ones
The traveling soldier
Thinks of getting home
The traveling soldier
Wonders what their family is doing
The traveling soldier
Wonders what all they have missed out on
The traveling soldier
Wonders if they will be able to go back to their old life
The traveling soldier
Wonders if they will ever live a normal life
The traveling soldier
Wonders if their bad dreams and memories will ever go away
The traveling soldier
Wonders if their family will recognize them
The traveling soldier
Wonders if their family and friends will still love them for who they are
The traveling soldier
Wonders what it will be like when they finally reach home
The traveling soldier
Can't wait till their traveling days are over

Trust

I trust you
When you tell me we'll be safe
I trust you
When you tell me we'll make it through
I trust you
When you're with other people
I trust you
When you make promises and try to keep them
I trust you
With all my heart

War Letters

Come from the heart of a soldier
To their loved ones
Come from a soldier
Who is in another country
Come from a soldier
Who thinks about home
Come from a soldier
Who dreams of holding the one they love
Come from a soldier
Who is fighting for their family
Come from a soldier
Who wonders if he'll ever make it home
Come from a soldier
Who isn't afraid to die
Come from a soldier
Who is loved and missed by their loved ones

Wedding Day

On our wedding day
We will get dressed up for our special day
On our wedding day
You will stand by the preacher waiting
On our wedding day
I will walk down the aisle until I get to you
On our wedding day
We will light a unity candle as a symbol of us becoming one together
with God
On our wedding day
We will face each other and say our vows
On our wedding day
We will take hands and will promise to love each other forever
On our wedding day
We will be announced as Mr. and Mrs.
On our wedding day
We will finally get to spend the rest of our lives together

When I Imagine You

When I imagine you
I see my best friend
When I imagine you
I see joy and laughter
When I imagine you
I see wonderful memories
When I imagine you
I see a beautiful life
When I imagine you
I see the most wonderful person in my life
When I imagine you
I see my partner for life

When I Saw You

When I saw you
I saw compassion
When I saw you
I saw God
When I saw you
I saw the love you have for your family
When I saw you
I saw kindness and gentleness
When I saw you
I saw happiness and joy
When I saw you
You took my breath away
When I saw you
You captured my heart
When I saw you
You stayed with me
When I saw you
I prayed and asked God if you were the one for me

When I'm with You

When I'm with you
You make my mind go blank
When I'm with you
You make my heart beat faster
When I'm with you
You drive away my fears
When I'm with you
You dry my tears
When I'm with you
You hold me tight
When I'm with you
You make me smile more
When I'm with you
You make me laugh more
When I'm with you
You say good morning to me everyday
When I'm with you
You say goodnight to me every night
When I'm with you
You tell me that you will love me forever

When We Say

When we say I love you
We get very excited
When we say I love you
We are the two happiest people
When we say I love you
We smile not only on the outside but also with our hearts
When we say I love you
We know we are the two luckiest people
When we say I love you
We both know we mean it
When we say I love you
We know that we are meant to be
When we say I love you
We both mean it with all our heart
When we say I love you
We know that we will always get to say it to each other
When we say I love you
We will say it until the end of time

When we're Apart

When were apart
We count down the days till we meet again
When were apart
We talk to each other everyday
When were apart
We try to make each other smile
When were apart
We try to make each other laugh
When were apart
We try to show our love to each other
When were apart
We tell each other that we are thinking of them
When were apart
We tell each other how much we miss each other
When were apart
We tell each other that we love them
When were apart
We will always be there next to one another

When we're Apart 2

We count down the days till we meet again
Because we can't wait to see each other face to face
We talk to each other everyday
Because we want to hear each other's voice
We try to make each other smile
Because it makes us smile
We try to make each other laugh
Because it makes us happy
We try to show our love to each other
Because it shows how much we mean to each other
We tell each other that we are thinking of them
Because we care about each other
We tell each other how much we miss each other
Because we really love each other
We tell each other that we love them
Because we are meant for each other

When You Come Home

When you come home
I get so excited
When you come home
I get to see my man after his day at work
When you come home
I get to see my best friend
When you come home
We get to spend time together
When you come home
I ask you how work went
When you come home
I have you relax
When you come home
I wrap my arms around you
When you come home
I give you a smile
When you come home
I give you a kiss
When you come home
I love to love on you

Who are You?

Are you the guy?
That works hard at everything
Are you the guy?
That enjoys the outdoors
Are you the guy?
That likes taking long walks
Are you the guy?
That likes to try new things
Are you the guy?
That likes to cuddle
Are you the guy?
That likes to smile and laugh
Are you the guy?
That loves to hug and kiss his girl
Are you the guy?
That makes sure his girl is loved and protected
Are you the guy?
That loves his girl with all his heart
Are you the guy?
Yes, you are that guy

Why Mom

Why mom
Did you not love me?
Why mom
Did you not want me?
Why mom
Did you punish me?
Why mom
Did you not want me in your life?
Why mom
Did you not want me to live?
Why mom
Did you not want me to be happy?
Why mom
Did you not want to see me?
Why mom
Did you not want me to have a family?
Why mom
Did you let them kill me when I didn't do anything wrong
Why mom
I was just a human being inside of you who just wanted to be loved

If your mother had an abortion with you how would you have felt if your life was taken from you without your consent?

Why Wait

When the one
That cares for you is always there
When the one
Loving you is trustworthy
When the one
That holds your hand is honest
When the one
That stands by you will keep you safe
When the one
You want to marry is the one you want to grow old with
When the one
Is in front of you and is there for you to grab a hold of

Will You

Will you
Take my hand and keep it in yours
Will you
Take your arms and always keep them around me
Will you
Take your fingers and run them through my hair
Will you
Look at me with those gentle eyes
Will you
Smile at me with that sweet smile
Will you
Talk to me with the voice that is so comforting
Will you
Take my legs and keep them in between yours
Will you
Rub your nose against mine
Will you
Softly kiss me on the forehead
Will you
Keep your heart next to mine

Won't Let Go

I won't let go
Because you are the one for me
I won't let go
Because you're my dream come true
I won't let go
Because I will always be there for you
I won't let go
Because you're the one I trust
I won't let go
Because you are sensitive and caring
I won't let go
Because I can see what's in your heart
I won't let go
Because you're the person I've been praying for
I won't let go
Because I want to always be by your side
I won't let go
Because you're the one I want to share my life with

You & I

You & I
Will always comfort each other
You & I
Will always hold each other close
You & I
Will always dry each other's tears
You & I
Will always walk hand in hand
You & I
Will always care for each other
You & I
Will always respect each other
You & I
Will always pray for each other
You & I
Will always thank God for each other
You & I
Will always tell each other how much we love one another
You & I
Will always be together
You & I
Will always love each other

You were the First

You were the first
To be there for me
You were the first
To make me really smile
You were the first
To tell me I was beautiful
You were the first
To wipe my tears away
You were the first
To chase my fears away
You were the first
To hold me tight and close
You were the first
To show me compassion
You were the first
To tell me how much you loved me
You were the first
To show me real love
You were the first
Person I've ever loved

You Wish

You wish
You could see what they look like
You wish
You could have the chance to hold them for the first time
You wish
You could touch their soft skin
You wish
You could hear then cry for the first time
You wish
You could give them a kiss on the forehead
You wish
You could tell them "I love you"
You wish
You could have taken them home with you
You wish
You could have watched them grow up
You wish
You didn't have a miscarriage

You

You mean so much to me
Because I trust you
You mean so much to me
Because you are the one whose there for me
You mean so much to me
Because you are my best friend
You mean so much to me
Because you are the one God brought into my life
You mean so much to me
Because you are the only man I want in my life
You mean so much to me
Because you are the love of my life

You're Love

Your love
Is unique and genuine
Your love
Is something that can't be completely described
Your love
Overflows your heart
Your love
Is like a rare gem
Your love
Is something I always want to have
Your love
Is like a secret I want to keep to myself
Your love
Is like the stars because they're never ending
Your love
Is something that should be cherished

You're My

You're my best friend
Because I can go to you about anything
You're my match
Because you are my other half
You're my marine
And you are my hero
You're my knight in shining armor
Because I'm safe when I'm with you
You're my first love
And my only love
You're my guy
And I'm the luckiest girl in the world
You're my sweetheart
Because you have a wonderful heart
You're my prince
And I'm your princess
You're my answered prayer from God
Because he knew we were meant to be
You're my every thing
And I would do anything for you
You're my honey
Because you are so sweet
You're my teddy bear
Because I love to cuddle with you
You're my lover
Because I love you with all my heart
You're my future
And I can't wait to spend the rest of my life with

You're my frog
And no one will ever love you as much as I do
You're my one and only true love
And you will be forever and always

You're the One

You're the one
I want to comfort
You're the one
I want to hold hands with
You're the one
I want to be there for
You're the one
I want to make happy
You're the one
I want to help when you fall
You're the one
I want to love forever